VEHICLES
ON THE JOB

PLOWS AND RIPPERS ON THE FARM

by Samantha Bell

Cherry Lake Press

Published in the United States of America
by Cherry Lake Publishing
Ann Arbor, Michigan
www.cherrylakepublishing.com

Reading Adviser: Beth Walker Gambro, MS, Ed., Reading Consultant, Yorkville, IL
Content Adviser: Louis Teel, Professor of Heavy Equipment Operating, Central Arizona College

Photo Credits: © Vevchic/Shutterstock, 3xy/Shutterstock, cover, title page; © True Pixel Art/Shutterstock, 4; © New Holland Agriculture, 6; © bbbb/Shuttestock, 8; © Luce Morin/Shutterstock, 10; © Design Pics Inc/Alamy Stock Photo, 12; © ilter42/iStock.com, 16; © oticki/Shutterstock, 18; © Smileus/Shutterstock, 20

Cherry Lake Press is an imprint of Cherry Lake Publishing Group.

Library of Congress Cataloging-in-Publication Data has been filed and isavailable at catalog.loc.gov

Cherry Lake Press would like to acknowledge the work of the Partnership for 21st Century Learning, a Network of Battelle for Kids. Please visit Battelle for Kids online for more information.

Printed in the United States of America

Note from Publisher: Websites change regularly, and their future contents are outside of our control. Supervise children when conducting any recommended online searches for extended learning opportunities.

TABLE OF CONTENTS

4

TIME TO TILL

Farmers plant **crops**.
First they **till** the soil.

Farmers till with **plows** and **rippers**. A tractor pulls them.

CONNECT

What other farm tools can a tractor pull?

8

PLOW POWER

There are different types of plows. A disk has a round shape.

A plow turns the soil over. It pushes weeds under the soil.

LOOK

See how the grass is getting turned over by the plow? It brings the fresh soil to the top!

Big tractors pull big plows. A moldboard plow also turns over the soil. Farmers use different plows for different soil.

RIP IT UP!

A ripper cuts into the soil, too.
It can go very deep.

The ripper makes the soil loose. **Roots** grow better in loose soil.

THINK

Why do you think roots grow better in loose soil?

TIME TO PLANT

The soil is ready.
Farmers plant seeds.

The new crop will be
growing soon!

FIND OUT MORE

Go online with an adult to find videos of plows and rippers. Write down some things you **see** and **hear**.

Then, write what you **think** about those things. **Make a connection** to something else you know.

Next, write what you **wonder** about plows and rippers from the videos. What would you like to learn more about?

GLOSSARY

crops (KRAHPS) plants that are grown as food or for other uses

plows (PLOWZ) farm machines used to cut, lift up, and turn over soil

rippers (RIP-urz) farm machines used to cut into the soil

roots (ROOTS) the underground parts of plants that take in water and materials that keep the plant healthy

till (TIL) prepare the soil for planting

INDEX

ABOUT THE AUTHOR

Samantha Bell has written over 100 books for children. She lives in South Carolina with her family and pets.